Your words are worthy.
Your voice is important.

PUBLISH **HER**™

PUBLISH HER SOFTCOVER JOURNAL

© Copyright 2020-2025 Publish Her Press

Printed in the United States of America

Published by Publish Her, LLC
6726 Walker Street
St. Louis Park, MN 55426
www.publishherpress.com

Publish Her is a female-founded publisher dedicated to
educating authors and elevating the words, stories
and writing of women.

PUBLISH **HER**™